FOR MY GRANDDAUGHTER SOFÍA RODRÍGUEZ
—SL

FOR MY PARENTS, STELLA AND JOSÉ, WHO TAUGHT ME
THE MUSIC OF SELENA, AND FOR MY BROTHERS, CLARA,
LAURA, AND JUAN, WITH WHOM I GREW UP DANCING
TO THE RHYTHM OF "BIDI BIDI BOM BOM"
—PE

 little bee books

New York, NY
Text copyright © 2020 by Silvia López
Illustrations copyright © 2020 by Paola Escobar
Manufactured in China   RRD 0122
First Edition 10 9 8 7
ISBN 978-1-4998-1142-1
Library of Congress Cataloging-in-Publication Data is available upon request.

littlebeebooks.com

For information about special discounts on bulk purchases,
please contact Little Bee Books at sales@littlebeebooks.com.

QUEEN of TEJANO MUSIC

SELENA

BY SILVIA LÓPEZ

ILLUSTRATED BY
PAOLA ESCOBAR

little bee books

LAKE JACKSON, TEXAS — 1977

The music coming through the window caught six-year-old Selena Quintanilla's attention. She bounded indoors and raced through the kitchen, startling her mother, Marcella.

"Where are you going, Seli?" Marcella asked.

"To sing with them, Mami," replied Selena. "They sound good!"

In the living room, big brother, A. B., strummed a guitar while nine-year-old Suzette beat rhythm on the drums. Their father, Abraham, had spent weeks teaching his older children to play their instruments. It hadn't always gone well. The kids often complained about practicing. They'd rather be out in the bright Texas sunshine! But that day, they were hitting all the right notes of "Blue Moon," a tune Selena knew.

Using a hairbrush as a pretend microphone, Selena burst into song. She had been singing almost since she could talk. Abraham, a musician himself in his younger days, listened more closely. His little girl had perfect pitch!

And as Selena twirled and danced in step with the music, something else became clear.

Selena was a performer.

THE QUINTANILLAS

Years earlier, on Easter Sunday, April 16, 1971, Marcella and Abraham Quintanilla had thought their third child would be a boy. A mom-to-be sharing the hospital room had picked a lovely name for her own baby, certain it was a girl. In a twist of fate, that mom had a boy. At a loss for girl names, Marcella borrowed the other mom's original choice: Selena, which means "moon goddess."

With a growing family, Abraham put away his music dreams and took a job with a chemical company in Lake Jackson, Texas. It was a good place to live. People of different ethnic groups got along well. Some were Hispanics—or Latinos—mostly Mexican American Tejanos, like the Quintanillas.

Neighbors remembered the Quintanilla children as happy and respectful. Selena seemed to have "something magical." She had a smile bigger than life and a voice to match.

Selena sang at family gatherings.

She sang while walking to and from school.

She sang to her classmates at recess.

"Selena was a good student who could go far," said one teacher. "She could win a college scholarship."

A FAMILY BAND

Music was always important to the Quintanillas. By 1980, they had formed a small band called Southern Pearl. The children practiced every day on secondhand equipment in the garage. The walls were lined with carpet pieces so rehearsals wouldn't bother the neighbors.

"My children are all talented," Abraham said proudly. "And Selena has stage presence." He arranged the music and booked performances at parties and country fairs. Everybody helped.

"My mom painted empty coffee cans black to make spotlights!" Selena said.

In 1980, Abraham quit his job to open a Mexican-style restaurant called Papagayo's. The band performed there most weekends. Imitating her favorite American pop artists, nine-year-old Selena's clear, strong voice soared over the clatter of dishes.

Then, in the early 1980s, the Quintanillas' life took a turn.

CORPUS CHRISTI, TEXAS – 1983

Times were tough in America. Jobs were hard to come by. People had less money to eat in restaurants. Papagayo's closed. The small house in Lake Jackson, including the furniture, was sold to pay bills.

The family moved to Corpus Christi, Texas. They rented a house in the Molina barrio, a middle-class neighborhood where many Tejanos lived. For Selena, everything changed—except making music. But now it became a way for her family to earn a living.

"We had no other alternative to make money," Selena said. With her as the main attraction, the band took the name Selena y Los Dinos—"Selena and the Boys."

Selena tried to look older than her twelve years. She wore makeup and flashy homemade clothes, but only onstage. At home, she was just like any other kid, although maybe more sheltered than most because Abraham was very strict.

In any case, there was little time for socializing, since Selena was often busy rehearsing or performing.

TOURING THE COUNTRYSIDE

Most gigs—or bookings—took place on weekends. Everyone, from extra musicians to the family dog, traveled in an old van together.

"Every time we turned, I rolled off the seat," Selena said, laughing.

Money was still tight for the Quintanillas. The family traveled from town to town, either sleeping in their van or at inexpensive motels. The money earned went to buy food from roadside stands.

"You have to take what you can get when you're getting started," Selena said. "We ate lots of hamburgers and shared everything."

If only a handful of people came to watch, the band still played their best. Those people had paid, and they deserved a good show.

THE LANGUAGE CHALLENGE

On the road, Abraham noticed that many people asked for Tejano music, also called "Tex-Mex."

Like the Tejano people, Tejano or Tex-Mex music has a character all its own. And it is sung in Spanish, which was a problem for the Quintanilla children, who were born and raised in the US.

They understood the language, but didn't speak it well. If the band was to succeed, Selena had to learn to at least *sing* in Spanish.

"I can't, Papi," she complained. "I don't know what all the words mean."

Abraham wrote down how the words sounded . . . and Selena memorized them. Soon, she was singing in Spanish with lots of feeling and no American accent.

The audience was convinced she knew what she was saying!

NO PLACE FOR A GIRL

As a girl lead singer, Selena faced another obstacle. In the Tejano tradition, performers had always been male. Some places refused to book the band.

"People told my father we would never make it," Selena said. "I wanted to prove them wrong."

Selena's brother, A. B., had learned much about composing and arranging music. He began writing new Tejano songs with a more modern beat. Young fans, especially girls, loved the fun dance steps Selena created.

LONG-DISTANCE SCHOOL

In 1985, Selena y Los Dinos recorded their first album with a small Texas company. Radio stations liked it, and the band got new gigs. But this created another problem: Selena was only fourteen years old. Traveling meant that she often missed school. The family couldn't afford to pass up any bookings, so Selena had to leave school in eighth grade. Right away, she enrolled in long-distance classes, studying while on the road. Everyone pitched in to help with lessons.

TELEVISION SUCCESS

In 1985, Selena y Los Dinos was also invited to be on a friend's television show. The band's lively new Tejano rhythm and flashy outfits were a success. It brought bookings at more important events. Still, much of the money went to pay for equipment and travel. Whatever was left was divided equally.

"If we got five or ten dollars," Selena said, "we could go to Whataburger!"

OFFSTAGE

In her spare time, Selena decorated her costumes with pearls, rhinestones, and lace. Some of the outfits showed off her figure. At first, her dad was not happy. The music of Selena y Los Dinos celebrated family values. Abraham didn't approve of drinking, drugs, or bad language. He didn't want his daughter giving the wrong impression.

"People like to see fancy costumes in the shows, Papi," Selena assured him. "They know who I really am inside."

Offstage, Selena led a quiet life. After performing, she stayed in the band's new bus—nicknamed Big Bertha—sewing, studying, or working on songs. She wasn't a typical teen. There were no school dances or football games. She never went out on dates. Her life was all about making music.

"I never had the opportunity to associate with anybody my own age," she said. Her friends were her family, band members, and people involved with their performances.

A RISING STAR'S CHANCE TO SHINE

Selena's first big recognition came in 1986. The band was nominated for a Tejano Music Award, an important prize. Although they didn't win, Selena, age fifteen, won Female Vocalist of the Year. She went on to win this and many other awards year after year. The Tejano girl lead singer had proven everyone wrong. Her star was on the rise.

"Always believe that the impossible is possible" became one of her favorite sayings.

In 1988, Coca-Cola wanted to make a commercial featuring Latinos. An executive invited several famous performers to record, but after Selena's audition, it was decided she would do it alone. The ad, recorded in English and Spanish versions, showed Selena's talent to TV audiences across America.

At seventeen, Selena was a lovely young woman, proud of her Hispanic heritage and her appearance. She wanted other Latina girls to feel good about their looks, too.

Her personality also impressed those she worked with. "She was wonderful to everybody. She remembered their names . . . and went out and hugged them," an executive said.

Soon after, Selena y Los Dinos were offered a big recording contract. The band turned out a string of hit songs. Crowds flocked to their concerts, thrilled with the new techno sounds and flashing lights. But the main attraction was always Selena's huge personality. Fans called her the Queen of Tex-Mex.

Selena never disappointed. "Be at your best at all times" was her motto.

CHRIS PÉREZ

In 1989, a young musician named Chris Pérez joined Los Dinos. He and Selena fell in love. Abraham thought Selena was too young for a serious boyfriend. But for the first time in her life, Selena opposed her father's wishes. She married Chris in 1992. As time passed, Abraham realized Selena had chosen well and welcomed Chris into the family.

FANS ACROSS THE BORDER

Tejano music hadn't been very popular in Mexico before Selena. But as her fame grew, fans there flocked to the band's sold-out concerts. Mexican newspapers, radio stations, and TV shows wanted to interview her. Selena had worked hard on her Spanish. It was good enough for singing—but was it good enough for interviews?

In 1992, Selena arrived in Mexico to face thirty-five reporters all eager to ask questions. She flashed the group a dazzling smile. She hugged each of the writers. When she made a mistake, she giggled. Please excuse my Spanish, she said. She was trying hard to learn the language of her songs. The language of her ancestors.

The reporters appreciated Selena's honesty and effort. They found her to be a "refreshing change" from other stars. Selena was clearly "one of their own, brown and proud."

"An artist of the people," one newspaper wrote. Selena was truly an international celebrity.

GIVING BACK

Selena never forgot her early struggles and those of her family. She began to reach out to the community, especially children, visiting schools to speak out against drugs and to praise the value of education. She gave money from her concerts to many charity organizations. Selena wanted to help young people achieve their dreams.

She also focused on some dreams of her own.

MORE SUCCESSES

Selena loved designing clothes. Why not open a shop to sell her creations?

In 1994, the first Selena, Etc. store opened in Corpus Christi, followed by another in San Antonio, Texas. Both were very successful.

In fact, 1994 was a year filled with successes.

The song "Bidi Bidi Bom Bom," which Selena helped write, became wildly popular. The catchy tune was constantly played on the radio. Then in March, her album *Live* was named Best Mexican American Album at the 1994 Grammy Awards. It was the first time that a Tejano woman ever achieved such a huge honor! Of course, Selena was very excited. But she was also excited to be among many big-name stars. Like any other fan, she went around snapping photos of the night's big winners, including Whitney Houston and Gloria Estefan!

SINGING IN ENGLISH

Selena had loved American pop songs as far back as her little-girl days of singing "Blue Moon" in the living room. But for years, producers would not offer Selena y Los Dinos contracts. They thought audiences might not listen to a Latino group performing American music.

It was different now.

Selena already had thousands of Spanish-speaking fans. The Grammy Awards got the attention of the rest of America. Wanting to be an entertainer for all audiences, Selena began work on a "crossover" album.

It was a bittersweet decision. Selena was now going to be a solo singer. A. B., Chris, and the other band members would help create and produce the music. But from then on, it wouldn't be Selena y Los Dinos anymore.

By early 1995, Selena had recorded several songs in English. When the album *Dreaming of You* was released in July, 1995, it sold 175,000 copies in a single day. A record for a female singer! Eventually, millions of copies were sold around the world.

SELENA'S GIFT

People who met Selena Quintanilla described her as sincere, humble, and gracious. "She stood in a class by herself," one person said, a reminder "to all Tejanos, all Mexican Americans . . . all Latinos, that theirs is a beautiful culture with a beautiful language."

Selena was a trailblazer. Her brilliant success opened doors for other Latino entertainers. She proved that talent and hard work could overcome obstacles and knock down barriers. She set an example for many young artists to follow.

Selena's life has served as an inspiration for Latina girls. She was a symbol of the power of family, determination, and pride in one's heritage. Her life is a reminder that all girls with big dreams can strive to reach their goals no matter who they are or what those goals may be.

The Queen of Tex-Mex lived her ideal of being at her best at all times.

And proved that the impossible is indeed possible.

1971

Born on Easter Sunday, April 16, in Lake Jackson, Texas, to Abraham and Marcella Quintanilla.

1983

Moved with her family to Corpus Christi, Texas. Learned to sing in Spanish by sounding out the words.

1985

Made her first recording for a local company. The band appeared on the Johnny Canales TV show.

1987

Won Female Entertainer of the Year at the Tejano Music Awards. Went on to win nearly every year until 1997.

1980

Sang with the family band, Southern Pearl, at Abraham's restaurant, Papagayo's.

1984

Left middle school to tour with the band, now called Selena y Los Dinos. Began homeschool classes.

1986

Won Female Vocalist of the Year at the Tejano Music Awards.

1988

Recorded Coca-Cola commercial. Became a spokesperson for the company.

1990

Finished long-distance courses and earned high school diploma.

1994

Won a Grammy Award. Opened fashion boutiques called Selena, Etc. in Corpus Christi and San Antonio, Texas. Began recording songs in English for her crossover album.

1995
March 31

Two weeks before her twenty-fourth birthday, Selena lost her life during an argument with an employee and former friend over the boutiques' finances.

1995
July 31

Selena's crossover album, *Dreaming of You*, was released. "Bidi Bidi Bom Bom" was chosen as Song of the Year at the Tejano Music Awards.

1992

Married Chris Pérez. Performed at sold-out tours in Mexico.

1995
January - February

Held a sold-out concert at the Houston Astrodome. Nominated for a second Grammy Award

1995
April 16

George W. Bush, then-Texas state governor, declared this Selena Day.

1997

The movie *Selena*, starring Jennifer Lopez, opened in theaters.

A LITTLE MORE ABOUT...

TEJANOS

After Christopher Columbus arrived in the New World in 1492, Spain claimed much of the land and began creating settlements. Later, these settlements became independent countries. Mexico is one such country.

At one time, Mexico covered part of what is now the southwest United States, including Texas. Mexican citizens had many different backgrounds. Beside Spaniards and Native Americans, there were people from Germany, Poland, and other parts of Europe. Some moved to Texas when it was part of Mexico, bringing along their culture. They stayed in Texas when it became part of the US in 1845. The descendants of those residents of the new state, like Selena's family, have been there for over one hundred and fifty years. They call themselves Tejanos.

HISPANICS OR LATINOS

Tejanos are part of a larger group of Americans, called Hispanics or Latinos, who have Spanish-speaking ancestors. Many of these ancestors came to the United States from South America, Central America, and the Caribbean islands.

Tejanos are no different from most other Latinos in the United States. They are as proud of their heritage as they are of being American. They might enjoy traditional food, sometimes called Tex-Mex, but also like hamburgers, pizza, and french fries.

Selena loved double-pepperoni pizza!

TEJANO OR TEX-MEX MUSIC

Tejano music is often also called Tex-Mex. It has a very unique sound. It blends American pop and country music with the original music of the different groups that settled Mexico long ago. Before Selena y Los Dinos, Tex-Mex music was not well-known in other parts of the United States. It took the catchy tunes performed and recorded by Selena and the band to make more people sit up, listen . . . and like it.

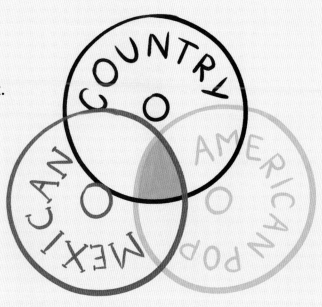

COUNTRY

MEXICAN

AMERICAN POP

▲ tex-Mex

QUINCEAÑERAS

When a Latino girl turns fifteen, her family often holds a big party called a quinceañera to celebrate her entrance into the grown-ups' community. But Selena was too busy rehearsing new songs, working on costumes, and traveling from town to town to make time for her quinceañera.

LAKE JACKSON, TEXAS

For the Quintanilla family, Lake Jackson was a good place to live. The town was made up mostly of people who worked for various chemical companies. There were Tejano and other Latino families, as well as Anglo Americans and people of different nationalities. For the most part, everyone accepted each other.

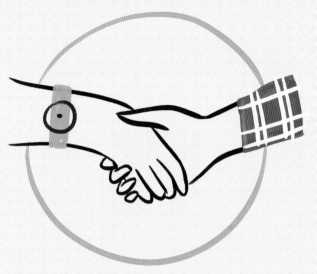

CORPUS CHRISTI, TEXAS

Corpus Christi, on the other hand, was a larger city and quite different from Lake Jackson at the time that Selena lived there. Families of different backgrounds usually did not mix. Tejano children did not attend the same schools as Anglo American children. Most Tejanos lived in neighborhoods, or barrios, like the one called Molina where the Quintanillas settled. Tejanos often faced discrimination. One college even had separate floors for Tejano students in its dormitories.

Yet, in Corpus Christi, Selena was surrounded by the warmth of her aunts, uncles, and cousins—part of her father Abraham's extended family. This helped when she gave up regular school in order to tour with the band. Touring meant giving up other things as well, like games, friends her own age, and holding a quinceañera.

SELENA BEHIND THE SCENES

During Selena's early years of performing, she didn't know the meaning of all the Spanish words she sang. It was a huge job for such a young girl to sound them out, memorize, and then sing—and dance—to them with feeling and emotion. She practiced over and over until the Spanish sounded right.

Besides all the effort she put into performing, Selena designed many of her costumes and those of the band. It was something she had always loved doing. As a little girl, she filled notebooks with ideas for doll outfits, then cut and sewed them out of fabric scraps. Purple was her favorite color, and many of the outfits she later wore onstage were purple.

When not hard at work, the Quintanillas shared a lot of laughter. Selena liked to play pranks. Once, she scraped the cream off Oreo cookies and filled them with toothpaste. Abraham ate one and said it was delicious!

TRAGEDY

Yolanda Saldívar had been one of Selena's greatest fans. In 1992, when she approached the Quintanillas wanting to create Selena's first fan club, she became its president and a trusted family friend. Eventually, Selena put her in charge of the fashion boutiques. It did not go well.

The facts about what happened on the morning of March 31, 1995, have never been completely clear. It is believed Saldívar may have taken money from the business and became angry when Selena confronted her. Yolanda Saldívar was tried, found guilty of murder, and sent to prison.

Selena's death was a terrible blow to Chris Pérez, as well as to her family and fans. Everyone was shocked and saddened. Cars bearing signs with sayings like WE LOVE YOU, SELENA! lined up for more than a mile outside the home Selena and Chris had bought next to her parents in the Molina barrio. Balloons, flowers, and toy Easter bunnies covered their front fence.

REMEMBERING SELENA

The Tejano world—and the whole music industry—lost a shining star with Selena's passing. In her short career, she achieved more than many other performers do in a lifetime. Joe Nick Patoski, who wrote her life's story, said, "The debate will never cease as to what could have been."

After 1995, the Tejano Music Awards continued to honor her accomplishments with a Lifetime Achievement Award, and TV's Univision bestowed upon her a Special Tribute Artist of the Year Award. In 2010, Selena was named the Female Vocalist of the 1980s and 1990s. "Bidi Bidi Bom Bom" was also named the best Tejano song of the 1990s.

Another award begun in 1995 is the Billboard Latin Music Spirit of Hope Award. It was created in Selena's memory and is given to a Latino or Hispanic performer for the charitable work he or she has done beyond the world of music. Perhaps, out of all the honors she received, this award would have pleased Selena the most.